Hymns and Classics

ARRANGEMENTS FOR THE ADVANCED PIANIST

BY GAIL SMITH

Contents

And Can It Be?	9
Hallelujah! What a Savior!	5
How Great Thou Art	26
In My Heart There Rings a Melody	18
Jesus Is All the World to Me	22
Just as I Am	35
My Faith Looks Up to Thee	33
Take My Life and Let It Be	13
Take Time to Be Holy	2

Copyright © 1982 by Lillenas Publishing Co.
All Rights Reserved.   Litho in U.S.A.

Lillenas Publishing Co.

KANSAS CITY, MO. 64141

Take Time to Be Holy

(In the setting of Chopin's NOCTURNE in E♭ Major, op. 9, no. 2)

GEORGE C. STEBBINS
Arr. by Gail Smith

Arr. © 1982 by Lillenas Publishing Co. All rights reserved.

Hallelujah! What a Savior!
(In the setting of Rachmaninoff's PRELUDE in C# minor, op. 3, no. 2)

PHILIP P. BLISS
Arr. by Gail Smith

Arr. © 1982 by Lillenas Publishing Co. All rights reserved.

And Can It Be?
(In the setting of Scarlatti's SONATA in A)

THOMAS CAMPBELL
Arr. by Gail Smith

Arr. © 1982 by Lillenas Publishing Co. All rights reserved.

Take My Life and Let It Be
(In the setting of Rachmaninoff's PIANO CONCERTO no. 2)

HENRI A. CESAR MALAN
Arr. by Gail Smith

Arr. © 1982 by Lillenas Publishing Co. All rights reserved.

In My Heart There Rings a Melody

(In the setting of Chopin's WALTZ in E minor)

ELTON M. ROTH
Arr. by Gail Smith

Copyright 1924. Renewal 1951 extended by Hope Publishing Co., Carol Stream, IL 60187. Arr. Copyright © in HYMNS AND CLASSICS by Hope Publishing Co. All rights reserved. Used by permission.

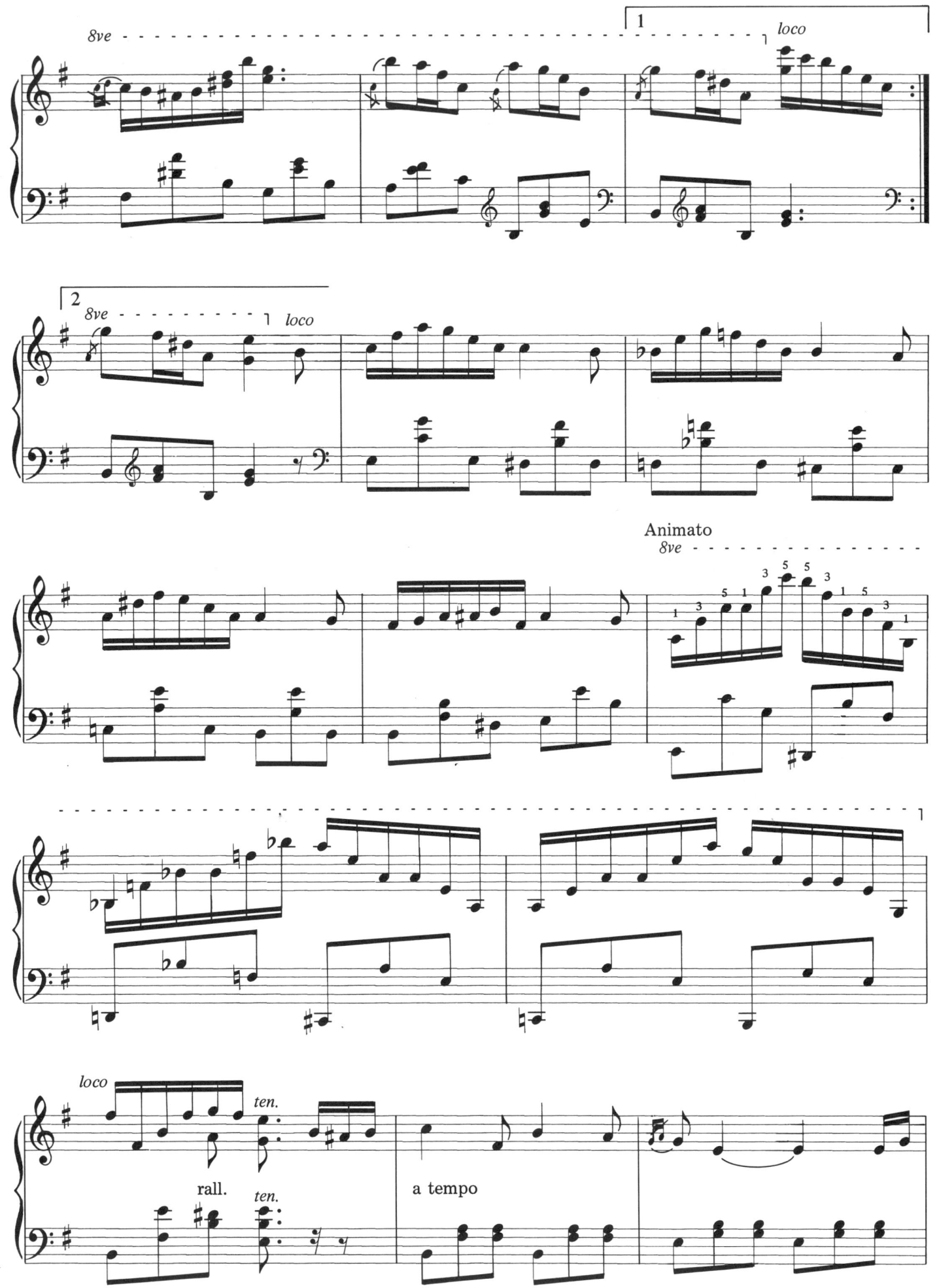

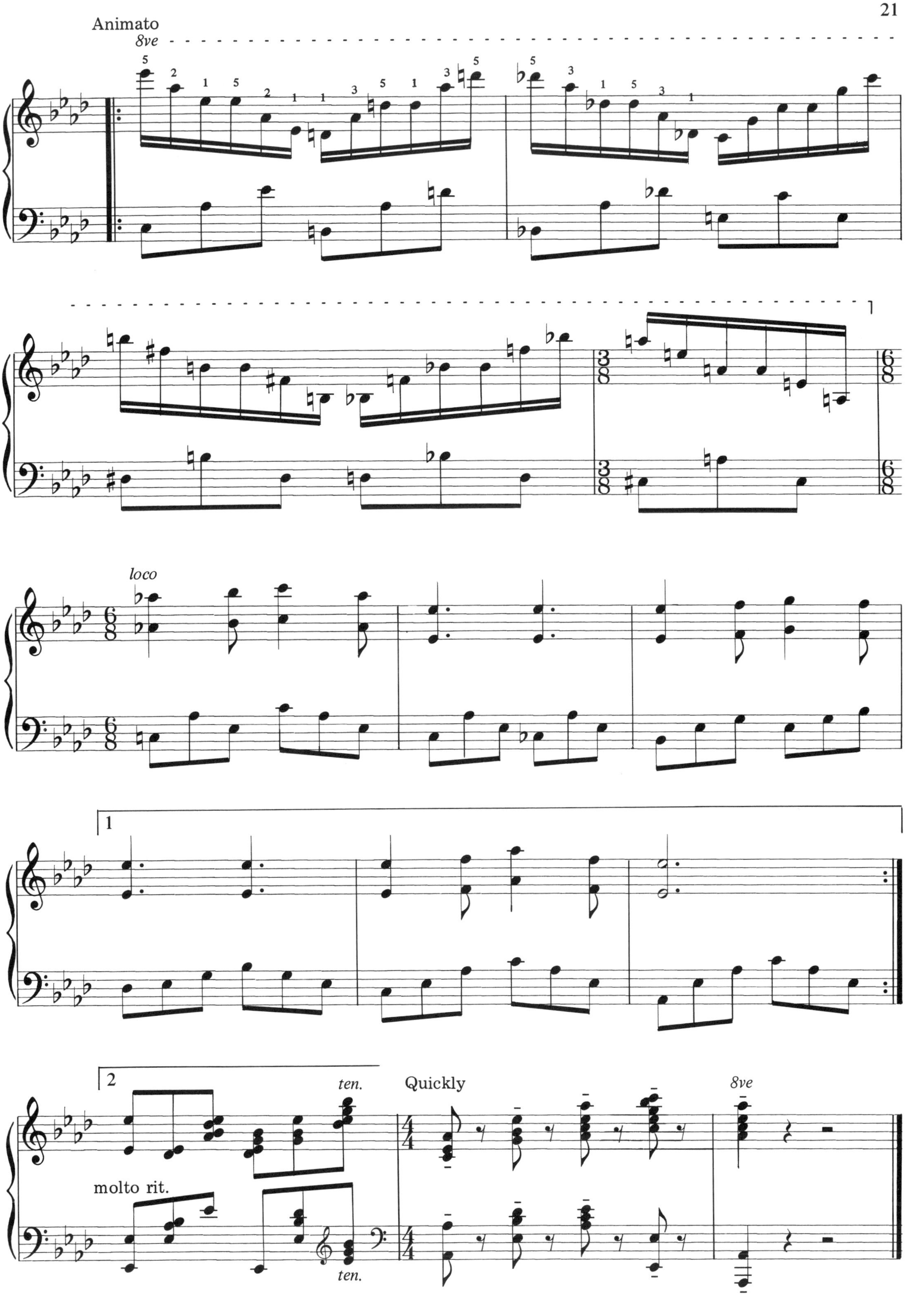
Animato
8ve
loco
1
2
ten.
molto rit.
ten.
Quickly
8ve

Jesus Is All the World to Me

(In the setting of Rubinstein's KAMENNOI-OSTROW, op. 10, no. 22)

WILL THOMPSON
Arr. by Gail Smith

Arr. © 1982 by Lillenas Publishing Co. All rights reserved.

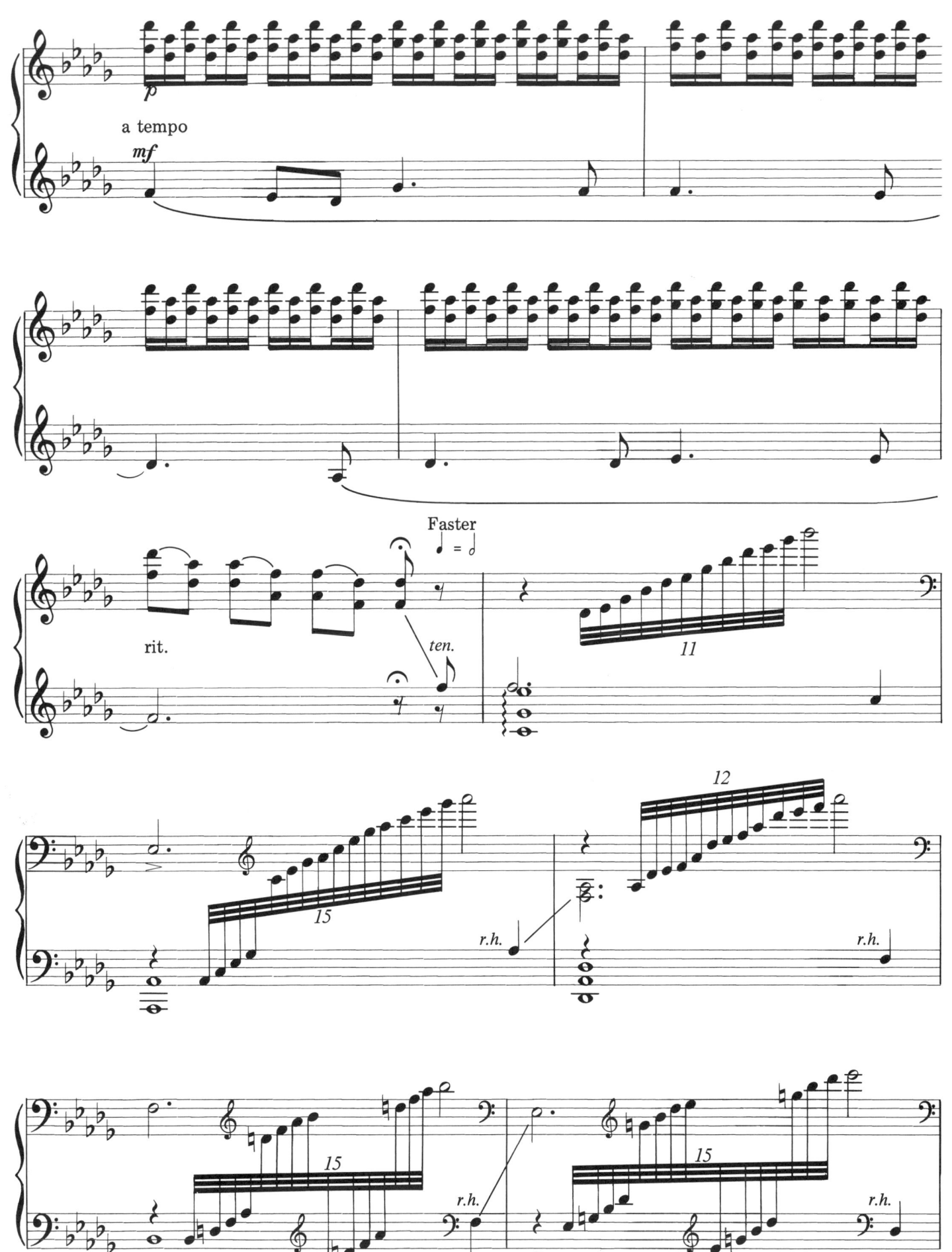

How Great Thou Art

(In the setting of Rachmaninoff's PRELUDE in G minor, op. 23, no. 5)

Swedish folk melody
Arr. by Gail Smith

Arr. © 1989 by Lillenas Publishing Co. All rights reserved.

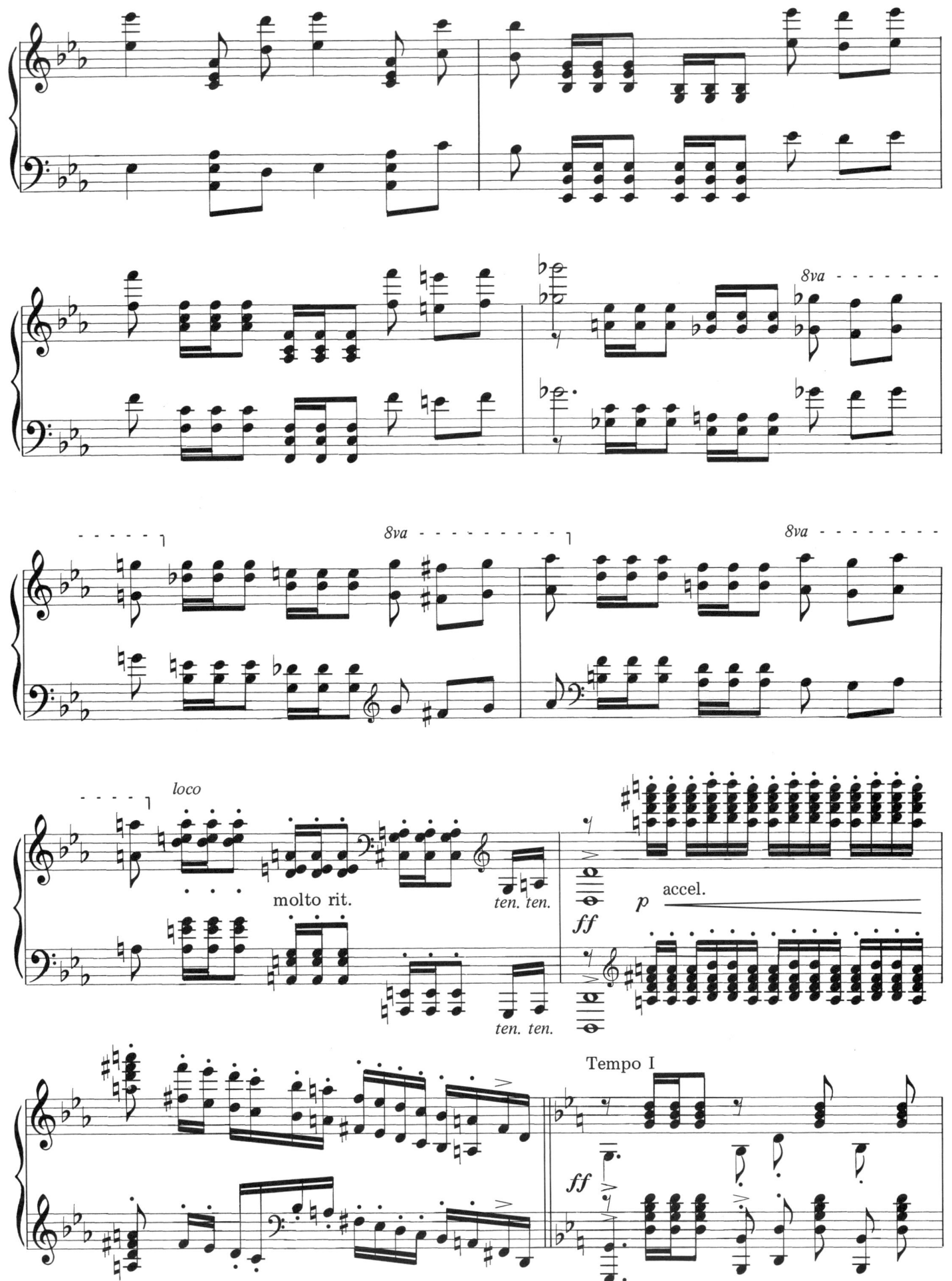

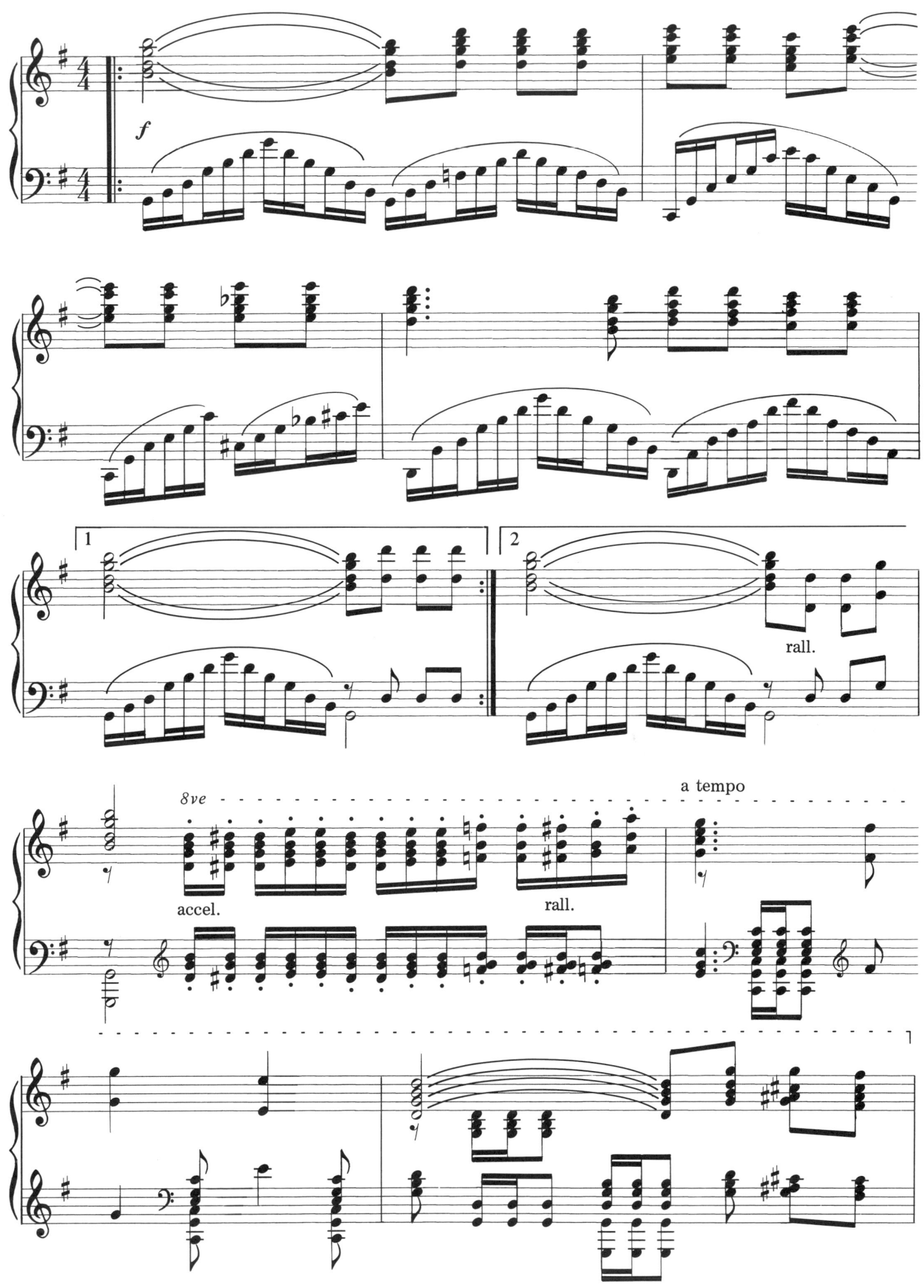

My Faith Looks Up to Thee

(In the setting of Mozart's SONATA, no. 1, in C)

LOWELL MASON
Arr. by Gail Smith

Allegro ♩ = 132

Arr. © 1982 by Lillenas Publishing Co. All rights reserved.

Just As I Am

(In the setting of Chopin's PRELUDE in A major, Op. 28, no. 7)

WILLIAM B. BRADBURY
Arr. by Gail Smith

Arr. © 1982 by Lillenas Publishing Co. All rights reserved.